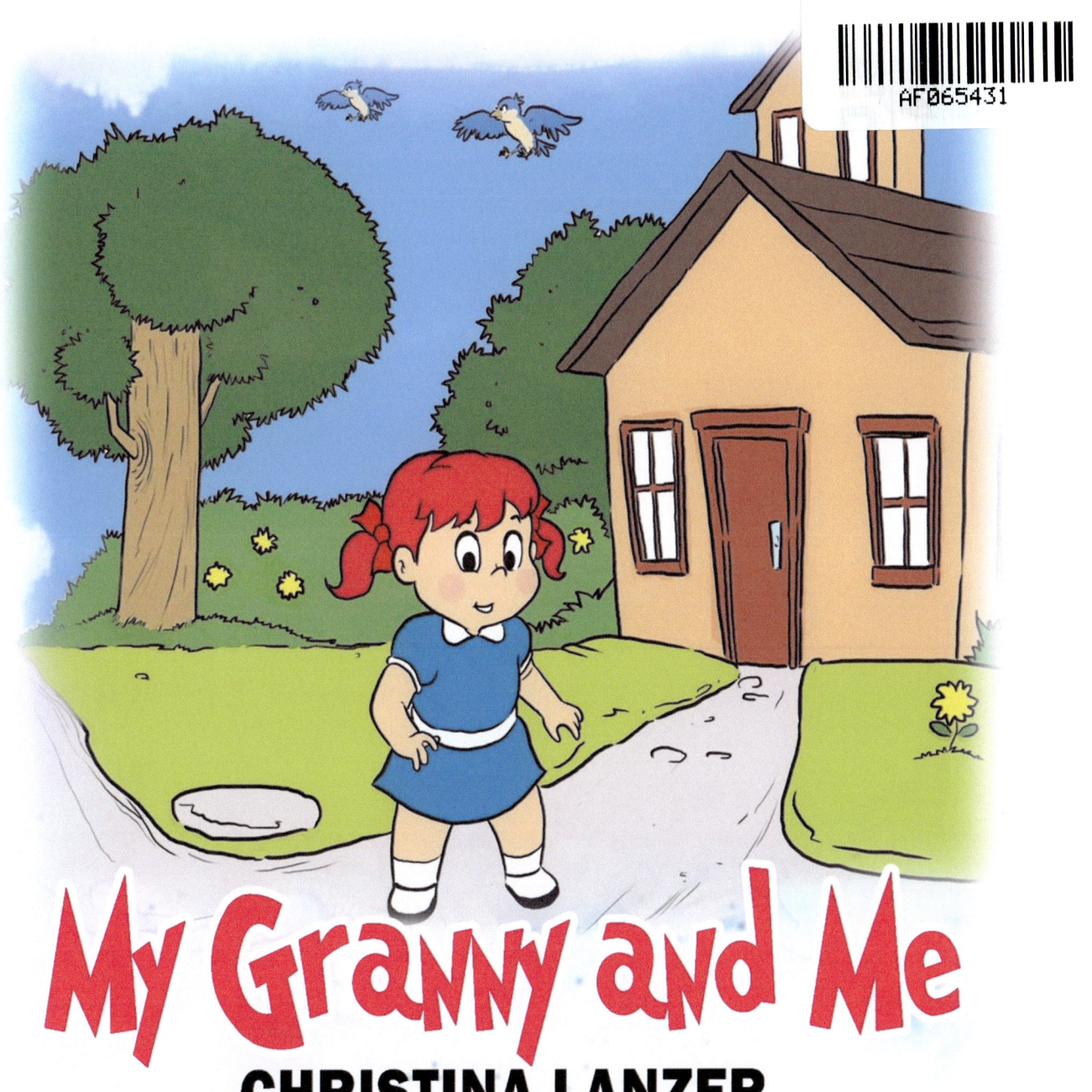

My Granny and Me

CHRISTINA LANZER

Copyright © 2022 **Christina Books**

All rights reserved. No part of this publication may be reproduced, distributed, or transmitted in any form or by any means, including photocopying, recording, or other electronic or mechanical methods, without the prior written permission of the publisher, except in the case of brief quotations embodied in critical reviews and certain other noncommercial uses permitted by copyright law. For permission requests, write to the publisher, addressed "Attention: Book Rights and Permission," at the address below.

Published in the United States of America

ISBN 978 1 958518 40 3 (SC)
ISBN 978 1 958518 41 0 (HC)
ISBN 978 1 958518 42 7 (Ebook)

Christina Books
222 West 6th Street
Suite 400, San Pedro, CA, 90731
mariejlanzer22@gmail.com

Ordering Information and Rights Permission:

Quantity sales. Special discounts might be available on quantity purchases by corporations, associations, and others. For details, contact the publisher at the address above.

For Book Rights Adaptation and other Rights Permission. Call us at toll-free 1-888-945-8513 or send us an email at admin@stellarliteray.com.

My Granny and Me

This is story about a little girl named Sara, who goes to her granny's house while her mother and father go to work.

Granny teaches Sara about different things each day.

Granny makes games out of the lessons, and together, they have lots of fun.

CHRISTINA LANZER

My name is Sara, and I am four years old. I love to visit my granny in her great big house.

I go to Granny's house when Mommy and Daddy go to work. We have a lot of fun, my granny and me.

Granny teaches me to say my ABCs and to count 1, 2, 3. We always have fun, my granny and me.

Granny teaches me to brush my teeth, brush my hair, and tie my shoes.

Granny puts my hair in pigtails and ties a big red ribbon around them . We always have fun, my granny and me.

On Monday, Granny plays outside with me. We play in the sandbox and make sand castles, my granny and me.

On Tuesday, I go to the grocery store with Granny. Granny lets me rided in the big shopping basket so I don't get lost. Granny lets me pick out the big red apples. When we check out, Granny lets me count her change. We always have fun, my granny and me.

On the way home, we stop at the ice-cream store. Granny buys us an ice-cream cone. Ice cream makes me giggle. We always have fun, my granny and me.

On Wednesday, Granny takes me to the zoo and teaches me about the animals. There are elephants. They are really big and have long noses. The giraffes have long necks and eat the tops of the trees. The monkeys swing from tree to tree. There are tigers, lions, bears, chimpanzees, turles, and lots of ducks and birds. We always have fun, granny and me.

On Thursday, Granny teaches me how to plant a flower in her graden. We plant marigolds, daises, and aster seeds. We water them, and Granny says the sun willl make them grow. We always have fun, my granny and me.

On Friday, Granny takes me to the movies. We get popcorn, soda, and candy. We always have fun, granny and me.

On Saturday, I visit my granny, and she makes me pancakes with maple syrup.

I help Granny make the beds and sweep the floors. I love my granny, we always have fun, my granny and me.

On Sunday, I go with my granny to church, where she teaches me to pray. I learn to listen and learn about my Heavenly Father, who loves me, and how he watches over us, my granny and me. We always have fun, my granny and me.

Illustration by
IVAN EARL AGUILAR

Printed by Libri Plureos GmbH in Hamburg, Germany